WAVES WITHOUT WITNESS

by

Daniel Van Vleet

Waves Without Witness

For permissions or inquiries, contact:

Waveswithoutwitness.com
inquiries@waveswithoutwitness.com

ISBN (Paperback): 979-8-9988595-1-9

First printing: 2025

This book presents philosophical and scientific reflections intended to inspire thought. While grounded in current understanding, all interpretations and conclusions are the author's own.

Table of Contents

Preface

Breath of Dust

You have breathed dust before. You just don't remember it.

The dust of stone. The dust of burned wood. The dust of cells you used to carry. The dust of ancestors ground down and carried on wind. The breath you took this morning contained pieces of mountains, of deserts, of forests long gone.

You are older than you think. Not in years, but in fragments. Every cell in your body is borrowed from something that once was. You are the brief convergence of uncountable forgotten stories.

And you will be forgotten, too.

This is not a tragedy. This is freedom.

Interlude

Bone and Water and Light

We are bone.
We are water.
We are light.

We are stories passed from firelit mouths to
broken stone, from ink to signal to vacuum.
We are the echo of heat in skin.
We are noise made fragile and temporary by
wind and decay.
We are here.

But not for long.

And that does not make us less.

Part I

The Illusion of
Importance

Chapter 1

Mattering

We all want to matter.

It is one of the first things we learn to want, even before we know the word. We want someone to notice when we enter the room. We want someone to remember our name. We want our presence to leave a mark, even a small one, that says we were here.

We carve our names into trees. We write in wet cement. We build careers, families, stories, and structures, not just to experience success, but to leave something behind that can speak for us once we no longer can. We chase legacy, not just happiness. We want to be known, and we want to be remembered.

That want is everywhere. It is in the pride we feel when someone says we did something well. It is in the warmth of being missed, even for a short time. It is in the need to share a photo, a story, a victory, a loss, anything that lets someone else carry a part of our life with them. Not because we are selfish. Because we are human.

We build things with our names on them. We hand our names down to our children. We build families not only to love and protect, but to carry something forward. Our faces, our names, our stories, our beliefs (pieces of us stitched into new people and sent into a future we will not live to see). Even when we do not know how to say it, legacy is often the reason we parent the way we do. And when we cannot pass ourselves forward through people, we try to do it through objects. We pass down watches, photographs, kitchen tools, letters, blankets. We turn ordinary items into vessels. We do not want someone to need the item. We want someone to want it. We want it to mean something. We want it to mean us.

Some of us gather others who want to matter in the same way. We start clubs, causes, cultures. We adopt shared identities and shared goals, not just for the strength of community, but for the hope that togetherness might insulate us from being erased. If we cannot be remembered alone, maybe we will be remembered as part of something larger. A movement. A generation. A name worth carrying forward.

Sometimes we aim to be unforgettable. We push harder. We perform. We make noise, not always because we need attention in the moment, but because we are trying to leave a shape behind that cannot be ignored. We compete. We excel. We build things large enough or loud enough or impressive enough that someone will have to remember us.

And other times, we do not need to be unforgettable. We just need not to be erased.

We just want someone to pause when they hear our name and feel that it still carries weight. We want someone to hear a story and remember that we were in it. We want to live on in a friend's memory, or a child's story, or a decision someone makes because of something we once said. Sometimes it is not about being seen by many. Sometimes it is about not vanishing entirely. A photo on a shelf. A name in a recipe. A line in a song that nobody else knows was about us.

The ache to matter is not weakness. It is a form of hope. Hope that our lives will outlast our time. That someone, somewhere, will look at what we built, or remember something we said, or smile at a story that includes us, and that for a moment, we will still be here.

We do not want to vanish. We want to be held in memory. We want to be remembered.

Chapter 2

The Fragility of Story

Stories are our armor against erasure.

They are what we pass down when we cannot pass down wealth. They are how we teach our children who they are before they have words for themselves. They are how we wrap memories in language so that they can survive just a little longer.

We tell stories to matter. We tell them to protect ourselves from the silence that follows when memory disappears. We tell them to outlive us, because they are the only parts of us that can speak after we are gone.

But stories are fragile. Spoken ones even more so. A single generation's silence can be enough to end them. A fire. A war. A flood. A shift in power. Sometimes a story ends simply because someone did not know to ask, or someone else did not know how to tell it.

Even the stories that do survive are not safe. They mutate. They fracture. They blend with other stories. The version that reaches your ear may no longer be the one that was meant to be told. Meaning drifts. The names change. The context gets lost. A lesson becomes a superstition. A warning becomes a proverb. A history becomes a myth.

We have always tried to protect our stories.

The earliest human stories are already lost. They were likely nothing more than grunts and gestures, rhythmic sounds passed mouth to mouth around firelight. They were simple patterns of meaning (this is danger, this is food, this is home). But breath is not durable. The moment the speaker vanished, so did the story. So we looked for something more solid.

From there, we entered the age of image. We painted on cave walls with blood, ash, and ochre. We recorded hunts, animals, signs, and dreams. The story was no longer fleeting. It could be seen by others, even after the fire died. But pigment faded, caves collapsed, and many of these paintings disappeared under earth or time. Images preserved more than sound, but they still failed to reach beyond a single place. We needed something we could carry.

Then came the age of symbol. We carved into stone and clay. We invented alphabets, etched ideograms, stamped ledgers. These were not just pictures (they were meaning with grammar, with order, with code). Now stories could stretch across generations. But stone broke. Clay cracked. Whole libraries of carved knowledge were buried, burned, or crushed under conquest. A symbol could last longer than paint, but it still needed a keeper. We wanted a way to copy.

Ink brought speed. The age of scrolls and script, of monks and memory. We copied myths and laws, genealogies and gospels. Stories traveled farther, and faster. But they still traveled slowly. Each copy required time. Each parchment was vulnerable to fire, to mold, to the silence of disuse. Knowledge became easier to destroy. We needed something that could multiply.

The printing press turned story into mass. We could flood the world with books. A story could survive because it no longer existed in only one place. But even then, the power to print was not evenly shared. Censorship still decided what deserved to remain. Fires still burned libraries. Wars still erased archives. Ink made story louder, but not invincible. We imagined a new kind of permanence; one built from machines.

The machine age brought us speed and access we had never imagined. Stories lived in silicon. They traveled as pulses of electricity. We encoded them into digital signals, stored them on servers, streamed them through satellites. The web offered something previous ages never could (the illusion of decentralization). Story everywhere. Instant. Indestructible.

We believed we had finally outrun forgetting.

But we were wrong.

Each age of storytelling gave us a better illusion of safety. But none of them made story permanent. Each only postponed the silence.

Stories remind us that we matter. We want that, and we need it. The pride we feel when hearing a story about ourselves is the peace of knowing that, at least for a while, we will not be forgotten. That we are carried. That our name still holds shape in someone else's mouth.

Stories are not just memories. They are boundaries. Shields. They define the edge between being remembered and being erased. And that is why we build so many ways to carry them forward (not just with ink or sound, but with ritual, with rhythm, with symbols, with repetition). We pass them again and again, like buckets of water meant to put out a fire just behind us.

But even the strongest story will eventually fall. A stronger story may take its place. Or time may simply push it out to make space for new ones. Most stories do not disappear in a single moment. They erode. They lose detail. They lose relevance. They are absorbed or overwritten.

Even when we try to tell them exactly, we cannot. Even when we mean to preserve them, we change them. And eventually, they will not be told at all.

The stories we inherit are only the ones that were lucky enough to survive. And even those are already rusting.

Chapter 3

The Dust and the Waves

Time does not move in straight lines. It folds. It presses. It crumbles.

Civilizations rise like tide-washed sandcastles, stacked in fragile confidence on top of forgotten attempts. One generation builds, the next forgets why it was built, and another starts again.

Cities fall into deserts. Forests rise over stone roads. Rivers change course and swallow whole communities without record. Some of the greatest structures ever built were erased before we even knew to look for them. Some were lost to wars, some to fire, some to neglect, and some to the quiet, patient persistence of weather.

We dig up fragments and try to guess what they meant. We hold bones and pottery and half-stories and pretend we understand their world. But we do not. We do not even know which stories were real and which were imagined. We do not know which details were sacred and which were incidental. We do not know if we are building on top of facts or misunderstandings.

Most things disappear without leaving anything behind. Most lives do not leave bones. Most settlements do not fossilize. Most stories do not echo long enough to be recorded. If you walked across the Earth looking for evidence of everything that has lived, you would find almost nothing (compared to all that was).

What survives is only what was lucky enough to harden in the right place at the right moment, or what happened to be remembered by someone who happened to be heard.

Even the strongest human creations fall apart. Stone erodes. Metal rusts. Mortar splits. No matter how carefully we build, the Earth breaks it down. Winds grind peaks. Rain carves gorges. Roots crack concrete. Oceans eat coastlines. Heat splits the surface of what once seemed unbreakable.

Nothing we build lasts longer than what will eventually break it.

The pyramids that remain are not whole. Their faces are worn, their interiors scavenged, their meanings debated. They are beautiful because they endured, but even they are fading. They too will be erased. It is only a matter of when.

All will be turned back into dust (like footprints on the beach).

The Earth does not remember us. It does not mourn our absence. It does not protect our monuments out of reverence. It never knew we were here. It may hold our scars for a while, but even those fade with time.

Plastics, which we once believed would last forever, will not even be artifacts given enough time. They will be broken down, scattered, buried, and burned. They are not immune, just slow to vanish.

We act as though getting rid of them is a favor to the planet. But it is really a way to stay longer. It is a way to not be pushed out by our own mistake. It is another kind of legacy. It is an attempt to be remembered for what we fixed instead of what we broke. But the Earth will not remember either.

And if the planet forgets us, the universe will never have noticed.

Chapter 4

Atmosphere of Forgetting

Not everything disappears in silence. Some disappear in noise. In friction. In heat.

Oxygen eats iron. Salt blooms beneath paint. Water expands inside stone. Roots find their way into brick. The slow movements of the world are neutral. They are destructive. They are constant. They do not stop because a story is meaningful.

Even when we try to protect what matters, the planet unbuilds it. Storms erase coastlines. Wind smooths names from graves. Earthquakes crumble what we thought was strong. Moss overtakes statues. Ice shatters glass. Heat warps and peels and pulls.

Everything built begins to decay the moment it is begun. Every wall is temporary. Every monument is a delay. Nothing we build can resist the elements forever, and the atmosphere is made of elements.

Plastics crack. Film curls. Tape unspools. Screens fade. Our new tools for preservation, like our old ones, are still vulnerable to time. Not immediately. But absolutely.

Waves are not only found on the ocean. They move through air. Through heat. Through pressure and light. The entire planet is shaped by cycles of motion, each one pulling a little more than the last. You can watch it happen on a beach. A single wave does not erase a footprint, but hundreds will. Thousands will smooth the sand. Millions will grind the shells into silt and scatter them out to sea.

The atmosphere is a sea too, only thinner. Less visible. But still full of waves. Wind and heat and pressure and radiation and movement. Each one pulls at what we make. Each one breaks something down. It does not happen all at once. But it always happens.

Radiation alters memory. Temperature corrupts code. Magnetic fields can wipe devices. We think of digital archives as incorruptible, but every technology we use to preserve memory has a lifespan. The materials themselves disintegrate. And often faster than we expect.

Even nuclear material, which we fear for its longevity, must be constantly contained and labeled. We bury it with signs that we hope someone will be able to read in ten thousand years. And still we know, the containers will fail. The labels will fade. The future may not recognize what we meant.

Time does not need to strike quickly. It only needs to continue.

The world we live in is not passive. It does not wait patiently beside our efforts. It applies pressure constantly. It peels. It breaks. It pulls apart. And all of it continues whether we are watching or not.

There are no pristine vaults. There are no sealed rooms untouched by weather. Even in the best conditions, air circulates. Molecules move. Temperature changes. Decay continues.

We like to believe memory is a kind of storage. That if something is remembered somewhere, it is still real. But memory is not a vault. It is a living thing. It must be fed, and repeated, and carried. And it fades. And it folds. And it fractures.

The Earth is not protecting our legacy. It is slowly removing it.

Fossils are rare. The preservation of any one thing is an outlier (a coincidence of pressure, temperature, sediment, and time). Most life leaves no trace. Most people are not found. Most cities are not uncovered. Most languages are never translated. Most voices are never heard again.

We do not just fade in history. We are erased by physics.

And that erasure has already begun.

Chapter 5

Fire in the Sky

The sun holds no memory of us.

Its light will burn across the surface of this planet long after we are gone. It will warm the dust where cities used to stand. It will rise over ruins, over cracked glass, over broken roads and rusted satellites. It will pull vines from the earth and stretch them across the bones of buildings. It will illuminate the quiet collapse without ever noticing that anything changed.

The sun does not mourn. It does not hesitate. It does not remember. It simply continues.

We often think of the sun as life giving, and it is, but not for us. We speak of it as a presence that watches over us, that feeds us with warmth, that rises and sets for our sake. But that story is ours, not the sun's. Its generosity is unintentional, and its violence is just as blind. Not deliberate. It gives because it cannot help but give. And it takes in the same way. Every ray of warmth is also a line of erosion. Every photon carries energy we cannot touch without cost. We depend on it to survive, but we cannot face it without being burned.

Every sunrise brings radiation. And with it, the quiet reminder that nothing lasting can ever come without cost. This same light that lifts our mornings also slowly unravels the evidence of our existence. It gives and it takes, without pause, without recognition. It is a rhythm that nurtures and erases in equal measure. Even on our calmest days, the light that feeds our plants, that colors our mornings, that warms our backs, is also stripping paint from walls, cracking skin, altering cells. The very light that sustains life is the same force that slowly breaks it down.

We were given a narrow window in which life could rise here, just the right distance, just the right angle, just the right atmospheric filter. Not by design. Not by intention. But by coincidence. And in the very same coincidence that allows us to exist, we are guaranteed to vanish. The sun, our giver, is also our undoing. The same light that grew the world will eventually erase all trace of us.

We try to filter it. We shade our eyes. We coat our buildings. We cover ourselves in fabric and formulas to delay its touch. But we are never beyond its reach. It touches everything. And it forgets everything.

Ultraviolet light does not discriminate. It fades paper. It cracks rubber. It bleaches stone. It carves itself into DNA. It destroys at the same time it sustains. It has no message. No intent. Only motion. Only energy.

Solar flares tear outward from the surface without aim. They blind satellites. They erase communication. They knock out power grids, short circuits, disrupt orbit. Not because we were targeted, but because we are fragile, and in the way.

We are incidental to its motion. Collateral to its flare. The sky above us is not a sanctuary. It is a flood of invisible force. We build towers to rise into it. We launch instruments to study it. We name it and thank it and design our myths around it. But the sun does not return the gesture.

It is not cruel. But it is not kind. It is not watching. But it is not blind. It moves without knowing. It burns without noticing. It will rise again tomorrow, and again, and again, long after our names are gone.

We look to the sky for hope, believing that what watches over us must also care for us. We search the heavens for permanence. For answers. But the sky offers none. Only light, only silence, only fire.

And in the end, the sun will burn away everything we ever tried to remember ourselves by. The colors of our flags, the letters etched in our monuments, the signals we sent into the dark. Our stories, our structures, our images, peeled away layer by layer, not with violence, but with indifference.

It will not remember us. It never knew we were here.

Interlude

Beneath the Structure

We built it high. Stacked brick on belief. Poured foundations of meaning into sand we did not test.

We thought the scaffolding was strength. We thought the height would give it permanence. But the rain has always found its way between the seams. The wind always learns the shape of every weakness.

And beneath the structure, beneath the effort and pride, the stone slowly splits. The iron rusts.

The stories printed on its beams begin to smear in the damp.

We built it anyway. Because building is all we know.

And when it falls, we will build again. Not because we believe it will last, but because the act of building helps us believe we were here.

Part II

Yielding and Entropy

Chapter 6

Carving Smoke

We do not build against time. We build inside it, knowing it cannot be held still.

Everything we make is shaped by decay the moment it is made. We try to carve meaning, carve memory, carve permanence, but we are carving into smoke.

And we know it.

We build institutions. Schools, governments, religions, treaties. They feel solid because we stack them on top of belief. But belief is fluid. It stretches. It sags under pressure. It dries out and crumbles. What begins as clarity becomes ceremony. What begins as unity becomes routine. And over time, even routine wears down into ritual that no longer remembers its origin.

We preserve ideas in systems. Charters, laws, scriptures, manifestos. We write with great care, believing that words will shield the meaning inside them. But words decay too. Their definitions shift, their references fade, and their tone becomes unfamiliar. Eventually, the words stay but the meaning slips through the cracks like breath from a cracked jar.

We maintain the illusion of order as long as we can. We patch failing structures. We reinterpret the past to justify the present. We rename things to keep them familiar. We confuse longevity with truth. But all of it is movement. All of it is smoke disguised as structure.

And the harder we press, the more obvious it becomes that we cannot hold the shape still.

A carved line in stone may last a thousand years, but even that surface will fade. Wind and water and time will blur its edges. A rule written in ink may be copied a million times, but if no one reads it, it becomes quiet and invisible. A belief may hold a culture together for centuries, but it only takes a few generations of forgetting to sever the bond that gave it life.

Entropy is not sudden collapse. It is quiet drift. It is forgetting made physical. It is the pressure that warps every archive, every building, every shared idea. The decay is not a single event. It is a process so slow and so constant that we call it normal.

And that is why we carve.

We know it will not last. We know we are shaping words, stories, values, into something that cannot hold its form forever. But we shape them anyway. Not because we think they will endure unchanged, but because for a while they give shape to us. For a while, they help us hold together, even as everything else begins to loosen.

To carve into smoke is to act even in the face of inevitability.

A child traces their family name into the side of a stone wall, something they believe will last. For a while, it does. Rain streaks down its face. Sun bleaches it. Wind grinds its edges. The stone begins to crumble, the letters fade, and eventually, there is nothing left but lichen and dust. No one remembers the child's name. No one remembers the wall. But for a time, it was there. Not because it was permanent, but because it was real, and witnessed, and offered the small, human joy of pressing meaning into something that felt solid. That is carving into smoke.

Even knowing the edges will blur, even knowing the shape will dissolve, we act. We speak. We build. We guide. We pass down what we can, hoping someone else will catch it before it scatters completely.

This is not foolishness. The value of being alive is to know something will fade and to do it anyway.

To carve smoke is to believe there is value in the act itself. In the effort. In the moment. Even if it disappears.

Especially because it disappears.

Chapter 7

The Earth is Not a Refuge

The earth does not protect us. It forgets us.

We live as if the planet remembers. As if it holds our memories in stone, as if it preserves our footprints in the soil, as if it cradles the fragile outlines of everything we have built. But the earth is not a vault. It is not a library. It is a system of erosion, collision, pressure, and change. It is built to move. And it has never stopped moving.

Continents shift. Plates collide. Mountains rise and wear away. Oceans open and close. Forests become deserts. Deserts become sea. What feels eternal to us is only temporary stillness in a much larger cycle.

Whole civilizations have been swallowed. Cities abandoned, not through war or neglect, but through drought, flood, volcanic ash, shifting rivers, collapsing soil. Sometimes nothing remains but the outline of a road or a few shards of pottery. And sometimes not even that.

The earth is not gentle with its surface. What we see as landscape is really scar tissue (bent, folded, cracked). The crust is always under pressure, always being reshaped. Mountains split apart. Valleys cave in. The ground rolls and shatters without warning.

We do not stand on solid ground. We stand on motion.

And that motion does not care what we place upon it.

We try to hold still. We try to root ourselves in place. We call places home. We build lives around coordinates. But the land beneath us is only borrowing that shape for a little while. It will shift again.

Pole shifts occur. The magnetic field weakens, reverses, reforms. Not often, but often enough to rewrite migration patterns, to unsettle weather, to confuse the orientation of life that depends on the quiet pull of north and south. We do not control that pull. We do not understand it fully. And when it changes again, it will not ask for our permission.

We try to catalog extinction events like they are history, like they are finished. But they are not finished. Extinction is ongoing. Some are sudden. Some stretch across millennia. Some begin so quietly that no one recognizes them until the absence is permanent.

The conditions that allow life are not guaranteed. They never were. We call Earth our home because it is where we appeared. But that does not mean it was made for us. We are not its purpose. We are simply incidental.

The planet does not hate us. But it also does not favor us. It behaves as it always has (through tectonics and climate and magnetism and storm). Its balance is not built on memory. Its cycles are not paused by our presence.

We dig deep to plant our monuments. We build wide to claim permanence. We pretend our maps are the final ones. But everything we have marked, every border, every building, every idea of permanence we have placed on this world will be broken down. Not because we were wrong to build them, but because this planet does not hold still for anything.

35

The pyramids are already weathered. Their faces cracked. Their inscriptions faded. Time and sand will wear them down as surely as it did the structures before them. Even they will become dust. Every mark we make will vanish.

The earth does not remember because it never knew.

We are not being erased by intention. We are being erased by motion. By pressure. By heat. By water. By the wind that does not ask what it touches. By a planet that moves forward with no need to look back.

We are not standing on a pedestal. We are clinging to a rock that does not know we are here.

And still we stay.

Chapter 8

A Star's Death

Even stars die.

Our sun is no exception. It will not burn forever. Its lifespan is long only by human standards. Astronomers estimate that it is just past middle age, with another five billion years before it expands into a red giant and swallows the inner planets. What follows is not fire, but collapse. The sun will shrink into a white dwarf, a glowing ember in the cold dark of space, slowly dimming over time until it no longer shines at all.

This is not tragedy. It is process. The end of a star is not a failure. It is a chapter. One that has been written into the physics of matter since the beginning. Our star is sustained by the fusion of hydrogen atoms at its core. When that fuel runs out, it will change. It will lose its balance. It will let go.

The atoms that make our bodies came from the death of other stars. We are only here because they were not. The iron in our blood, the calcium in our bones, the oxygen we breathe (all of it was formed in the heat and pressure of stellar destruction). Their deaths were not mourned. Their collapse was not observed. They simply became part of something else.

And we are just one more step in that process.

There is no ceremony when a star dies. No eulogy. No record. It simply changes. It becomes something else, something quieter. Sometimes, it leaves behind a nebula, casting gas and light across the void. Other times, it leaves only gravity. The last heat fades, and nothing remains to remember the flame.

We live in the warmth of our star and often mistake that warmth for affection. But the sun does not burn for us. Its energy is not offered. It simply radiates, indifferent to whether anything receives it. We interpret light as generosity, but the sun does not know that we are here. Its brightness is not a gift. It is the natural consequence of its mass and motion.

We teach children to draw the sun with a smiling face, as if it is watching over us. But the truth is simpler. It is not smiling. It is not watching. It is not waiting. It is doing what it must, as it has, long before we appeared, and as it will, long after we are gone.

There will come a time when the last human eye will close and the sun will still rise. The final breath will leave a body, and the morning light will still stretch across oceans and stone. It will not pause. It will not know.

We build calendars and rituals around it. We call it ours. We worshipped it once. But the sun has no memory of being honored. And it will not remember being forgotten.

In the end, even it will fail. Even it will fade. The warmth that held Earth in balance will flicker and go dark. And in the vast reach of space, that loss will mean nothing.

Not because it is meaningless, but because there is no one to assign meaning at all.

Interlude

Scale of Silence

The stars do not speak.
They do not ask for poems or prayers.
They do not echo our songs.
They do not send back messages wrapped in
light.

We look up and imagine meaning in their
shimmer,
but they do not shimmer for us.
They burn, fuse, and collapse,
following the same laws that forged them from
gas and void.

We measure distance in light years,
but rarely pause to feel what that means.
A whisper, shouted across billions of miles,
arrives far too late for anyone to hear it.

Silence is not emptiness.
It is scale.
It is the vastness between what exists and what
can respond.
And the farther we look,
the quieter everything becomes.

We are not ignored.
We are not punished.
We are simply smaller than we imagined,
and much further away than we ever hoped.

Part III

Indifference of the Stars

Chapter 9

Ghosts of Galaxies

Galaxies collide.

It seems impossible. From our perspective, these spiraling clusters of light seem fixed, eternal, untouchable. But in the dark fabric of space, everything moves. The Milky Way is hurtling toward Andromeda at hundreds of kilometers per second. Their meeting is not a possibility, but a certainty. NASA and ESA simulations estimate their collision will begin in roughly four billion years.

There will be no impact in the way we imagine. Stars are too far apart to crash like cars on a highway. Instead, gravity will stretch and twist the two galaxies, pulling them into new shapes. Stellar nurseries will awaken. Some stars will be flung into the void. Others will be captured by new orbits. What was once two will become something unrecognizable.

We often imagine galaxies as quiet, ancient cities of light. But they are restless. They are temporary. They are shaped by tension, pulled apart by gravity, consumed by time.

Some galaxies are already gone. Not vanished, but dismantled. Their remnants are scattered in tidal streams and faint smudges on the edges of other systems. We can still detect their ghosts, sometimes, through spectral signatures or gravitational echoes. But they are no longer what they were. Their names are gone. Their structure, erased.

We live inside one of these systems, orbiting a star that will also fade. We call our galaxy home, but it is only a stop. It is a structure made from motion. A temporary shape that forgets itself over time.

Black holes drift through the centers of galaxies, bending light, swallowing stars. They are not destroyers in the way myths imagined, but they erase all records of what enters. No message escapes. No history remains. The Event Horizon Telescope captured the first image of a black hole's shadow in 2019, giving us a glimpse of the mechanism behind that erasure. It is not mystical. It is not vengeful. It is silence wrapped in gravity.

We look out and see beauty. Swirling arms, glowing cores, clouds of gas painting themselves across the void. But what we are seeing is only what has not yet been pulled apart.

Even the Milky Way will dissolve. After its merger with Andromeda, it will become something new, perhaps elliptical, perhaps chaotic, and eventually it too will lose its shape. The stars will scatter. The structure will thin. And one day, there will be no more spiral to remember.

Nothing about this is unnatural. It is what galaxies do. Their light travels for billions of years, only to reach us at the very edge of seeing. And even that light is old. It is already a ghost.

When we look to the sky, we are looking into the past. Not poetically. Literally. The further we look, the older the light becomes. The deeper the silence. Some of the galaxies we see through telescopes are no longer there at all. They burned out, collapsed, or merged before we were born.

We see their ghosts. But they cannot see us.
And they never could.

We are not known by the stars we orbit. We are not kept in memory by the galaxies that gave rise to our elements. Their silence is not neglect. It is nature. Their indifference is not cruelty. It is the rhythm of all things moving through time. The universe has made space for us, but not meaning.

What we build, what we love, what we remember, all of it flickers here for but a moment, in the dark between stars. Long before we are gone, the places that shaped us will begin to forget.

Chapter 10

Heat Death and the Silence After

Physicists call it heat death. The universe expanding so far, for so long, that eventually all energy is evenly distributed. No gradients. No reactions. No stars. No structure. Nothing left to push or pull. Just cold, still silence.

This is not science fiction. It is a projection built from everything we observe about thermodynamics, background radiation, the motion of galaxies. The second law tells us that entropy always increases. The more time passes, the more things fall apart. Not just on Earth, not just in stars, but everywhere.

There will come a time when the last star burns out, when black holes evaporate into nothing, when particles themselves begin to decay. And there will be no light left to carry memory. No matter to hold shape. No voice to tell any story.

This is not punishment. There is no judgment in the cooling of the cosmos. Just a final breath that never rises again.

The expansion of the universe has been measured with precision. Every supernova, every galaxy pulled farther from the others, all confirm what we already suspect. The fabric of space stretches. What was once dense and burning is now vast and thinning. There is no force pulling it back together. No edge. No reset. Just distance. Just time. Just silence.

Even the fundamental forces will begin to fail. Gravity weakens across cosmic scales. Nuclear bonds lose their grip. And when the balance breaks, structure disappears. What we know as time may still unfold, but there will be no change left to mark it.

The energy that once gave rise to stars and planets, to thought and love and pain, will dissipate across a volume too wide to measure. Temperature drops toward absolute zero. Movement stops. Memory ends. Not in fire, but in stillness.

Some models suggest small pockets of temporary order might flicker here and there, quantum fluctuations rippling into brief shape before vanishing again. But even these are rare and brief. There is no future waiting in the cold.

We live in a warm chapter. A window. A brief flare in a timeline that stretches beyond comprehension. Our entire existence (every culture, every language, every birth and death) fits into a breath drawn between two phases of silence.

There will be no one to find our ruins. There will be no ruins to find. No one to hear our last words. Not because they were ignored, but because everything that could have listened is also gone.

The silence will not be cruel. It will not be triumphant. It will not even know it is silence. It will simply be.

We hope to be remembered, but the universe does not hold memories. It holds mass and motion and light (for a while). And then it holds nothing.

Chapter 11

Nothing Was Ever Ours

We build. We name. We declare ownership.

We place flags and fences. We title land and sea. We carve signatures into metal and stone. And we say it belongs to us.

But the Earth never agreed. The stars never signed. The universe never noticed.

Not even the atoms we are made of are truly ours. They pass through time, through bodies, through births and deaths and births again. What we call ours is only on loan. Our stories, our beliefs, our bones and breath, all stitched together from borrowed matter, stitched together just long enough to feel like a self.

It is easy to believe that ownership offers safety. That permanence can be held in a deed or a document. That a name engraved means a legacy secured. But nothing resists time. Not really. Not even stone lasts forever. Not even mountains stay still.

We do not own the sky we fly through. We do not own the soil we bury our dead in. We do not own the water that carves the rivers or the air that fills our lungs. These are gifts we were given. Not as rewards, not as inheritance, but as context. We were born into their motion, and we will vanish in their motion too.

What we build, we often believe we deserve. What we lose, we believe was taken. But perhaps nothing was ever truly held to begin with.

This does not need to be a tragedy. There is peace in recognizing that we are not keepers, but witnesses. That we are not here to preserve everything as it was, but to see it as it is. To understand it while we can.

To witness is not to control. It is to attend. To be present in the passage. To walk beside the river rather than trying to hold it still.

And in this role, there is clarity. We do not need to hoard or protect what cannot be kept. We do not need to fear the loss of what was never ours to begin with.

If we are here only for a moment, let it be a moment of seeing clearly. Of experiencing fully. Of understanding the strange beauty of being temporary in a world that never asked us to last.

None of this lessens the importance of stewardship. Witnessing does not mean turning away from responsibility. We still have choices. We still build. We still alter what we touch. And that influence carries weight.

But we are not stewards for the sake of legacy. We are not caretakers to be remembered. We are not saving the Earth. We are preserving our window within it, so that the next hands, the next eyes, the next voices, can also witness.

And maybe that is enough.

Not to own. Not to preserve. But to witness the wonder while it lasts.

Interlude

After the Edge

The ocean does not notice the boat.
The wave is not angry at the stone.
And still, we shout into it.
We name our ships.
We believe our maps.

But there is freedom in surrender.
In knowing we were never steering.
In seeing the horizon not as a limit,
but as a place to disappear.

Let the silence take what it will.
Let the tide erase what it must.
We are not here to last.
We are here to feel the water.

Part IV

Liberation

Chapter 12

Joy in the Temporary

Beauty is not less because it fades. It is more.

The cherry blossom does not weep when it falls. The snowflake does not beg for permanence. These moments, these glimpses of wonder, do not apologize for being brief. And they are no less extraordinary because they vanish.

We spend our lives under the weight of needing to matter. We chase the illusion of permanence in every plan, every achievement, every desperate attempt to be remembered. But none of it lasts. None of it was ever going to.

The world does not ask you to be important. The sky does not need your legacy. The universe does not care how well you played the game. And in that silence, there is peace.

It is not our job to be remembered. It is not our task to be impressive. We are here, for a moment, and then we are not. Nothing we do will slow the turning of galaxies or shift the tides of deep time. But we do not need to shift them. That was never our purpose.

This freedom is not emptiness. It is clarity.

If the systems of the universe do not care how much you accomplish, how clean your house is, how many hours you worked this week, how many people approved of you, then you are free.

Especially because it will not last.

We believe we must earn our worth through effort, through worry, through proving something to a world that was never keeping score. But the universe is not a judge. It is not watching. It is not keeping tallies or writing stories about us in the stars. It is a system of motion, of unfolding physics, of tides within tides, all moving toward balance with no regard for our presence.

And still, we try. Still, we wake. Still, we love.

Not because it changes the universe, but because it changes us.

The joy of living is not in building something eternal. It is in choosing how to spend the fleeting seconds we are given. If everything is temporary, then everything is precious. If everything is passing, then we can stop trying to hold it all, and instead simply hold what matters.

Our anxiety often comes from believing it is all up to us. That we are supposed to matter, supposed to fix everything, supposed to live the right way, choose the right career, protect every possible outcome. But the truth is that no matter what we do, the tides will come. The winds will shift. The world will turn with or without us.

You are not failing at life. Life was never meant to be held. It was only meant to be touched.

So breathe. Let go. Smile when the sun hits your face, even if the warmth is brief. Say yes to joy, not because it lasts, but because it is here now. You are not here to win. You are here to witness.

And that is enough.

Chapter 13

Choosing How to Burn

We do not get to choose whether anything vanishes. Everything we have ever touched, everything we have ever made, every word we have spoken, will vanish. The tides of this planet will wash it all away. The winds will scatter it. The sun will burn it. Time will forget it.

But we are still here now.

And for this impossibly brief moment, we get to choose what we do with that.

The wave is coming. It always has been. We do not control the water. We do not build the tide. But we are allowed to choose what we place on the sand.

So we build sandcastles and driftwood sculptures. We write messages in the shore. We throw stones just to see how far they go. We teach. We sing lullabies. We comfort our children. We plant trees we will never sit beneath. We keep promises. We say I love you, again and again, knowing that someday even the language will be gone.

We are not asked to last. We are asked to burn.

It's like lighting a match and setting it gently in a paper boat. You place it on the waves not to fight the tide, but to let it drift, glowing. You know the water will take it. That was never in question. But for a few seconds, it carries its light forward, a flicker of warmth across the surface.

There is no version of your life that will be remembered forever. Not through children, not through books, not through statues or foundations or great works. Nothing stays. But you can still shape how it goes. You can still choose how you spend what you were given.

You can spend your life trying to be remembered. Or you can spend your life making someone else feel remembered. You can spend your life building something that gives comfort. Or you can spend it creating moments so full of presence that memory does not matter.

This is not about giving up. This is about choosing your flame.

You can be the kind of person who stays late to clean up after the gathering no one will recall. You can be the one who pulls over on the side of the road to help a stranger carry their things. You can tell stories that make someone feel seen. You can build a small business with integrity. You can hold a hand through grief. You can plant a community garden. You can be kind when it is inconvenient. You can live gently with yourself. All of it matters, even if none of it lasts.

The light we give may not last. But it is still light.

If the universe does not care what we do, then we are free to do what matters most to us. Not for legacy. Not for perfection. But for meaning. For passion. For peace. For love. For joy. For the quiet sense of being alive and doing something beautiful with the time we were given.

You are not here to win anything. You are not here to be measured by someone else's scale. You are not here to fix the unfixable. You are not here to beat time. You are here to live.

Burn well. Burn bravely. Burn in ways that warm others. Burn in ways that illuminate your path.

Burn with the full knowledge that it will not last, and that it never needed to.

And when the wave finally comes, when the shore is empty again, let it come without regret. Let it come with nothing left unsaid. Let it come knowing you did not waste your fire.

You were never here to last.

You were here to burn something beautiful while it lasted.

Epilogue

What Is Left to Witness

If the universe cannot remember us, maybe we were never meant to be remembered. Maybe we were meant to witness. To hold the moment, however briefly, and let it move through us like light across water.

We are small. Infinitesimal. Not just in size, but also in time. Our names, our memories, even our greatest monuments will be worn away. There is no record that survives forever. There is no voice loud enough to echo in a silent universe. But this is not a reason to despair. It is the beginning of peace.

Because if nothing can truly be held, then nothing can truly be lost. And if none of it is permanent, then the weight we carry, the anxiety, the perfectionism, the fear of being forgotten, is no longer ours to hold.

We were given a short window. Not by design. Not as a gift. Just by coincidence. The right distance from a star that doesn't know our name. And within that coincidence, we found consciousness. We found beauty. We found each other.

And maybe that is enough.

We cannot force the universe to care about us. But we can care for each other. We can learn to loosen our grip. We can build lives rich in meaning even when nothing lasts. We can plan for a future we'll never see.

In the next volume, we will explore what it means to be part of a larger pattern. We will ask whether consciousness, memory, and meaning could stretch beyond the boundaries of our biology, not as faith, but as emergence. We'll look to the systems behind connection, the physics of pattern, the illusion of separation, and the real weight of witness

And after that, we'll ask what it would take to outlive ourselves. What we would need to become, not to be remembered as individuals, but to endure as a species.

The waves are still coming.

But maybe now we can learn how to ride them,
if only for a moment.

Further Reading

The following books, articles, and sources offer scientific grounding, conceptual expansion, or philosophical parallels to the ideas presented in this book:

The Sixth Extinction by Elizabeth Kolbert
A compelling exploration of biodiversity loss and human impact on the planet.

Sapiens: A Brief History of Humankind by Yuval Noah Harari
A sweeping narrative of human evolution and our role in shaping the world.

NASA Solar Physics Division by
https://science.nasa.gov/heliophysics
An excellent source of scientific insight on the sun and space phenomena.

Entropy and the Arrow of Time by Sean Carroll
A scientific dive into the implications of entropy on time and existence.

The End of Everything (Astrophysically Speaking) by Katie Mack
An accessible and engaging explanation of how the universe might ultimately end.

These references do not attempt to answer the unanswerable, but they do help frame the space where science and humility meet.

www.ingramcontent.com/pod-product-compliance
Lightning Source LLC
Chambersburg PA
CBHW071539120626
46550CB00006B/2514